Hindu Mythology

A Guide to the Gods and Goddesses of India

Table of Contents

Introduction

Hindu mythology is vast and features many gods and goddesses, most of whom have multiple variations of their names and associations. According to the Hindu religion, these deities were once human or superhuman beings. Some of them are still worshipped today as the gods and goddesses of the Hindu religion. In addition, many Hindus worship certain animals or objects that represent their deities.

The Origins of Hinduism

Hindu mythology first appeared during the Vedic Period, which was between 2300 B.C. and 1500 B.C. The essence of Hinduism is described through the Vedic literature that comprises the Vedas, the Brahmanas, and the Upanishads. Hindu mythology covers a vast amount of time and space, beginning approximately 3500 B.C., and continuing well into the 21st century A.D. The Hindu religion does not have a "Holy Book," like the Bible or the Koran which is seen as having been inspired by a divine being, but instead, is made up of many books written by various authors. The books that are considered part of Hindu mythology include the Ramayana, the Mahabharata, the Bhagavad Gita, and The Upanishads.

There are many Hindu deities, and they are inspired by human traits as well as aspects of nature. They are worshipped according to either their benevolent or destructive natures. Some of the most worshipped deities are Vishnu, Shiva, Lakshmi Devi, Ganesha, Krishna, Rama, and Kali. The word Hindu is derived from the Sanskrit word "Sindhu," which refers to the historical name for the Indus River in northwestern India. The Hindus refer to themselves as "Hindu", which is derived from the word "Sindhu." The historical context in which Hindu mythology appeared includes prehistoric cities in the Indus River valley.

At first, there was no definitive collection of Hindu myths because there were so many variations on each myth. Eventually, many areas merged their stories to create a more central collection, but not all regions agreed to what was included. This eventually led to the main collection of Hindu mythology that included stories about the creation of the universe, the origins of man, and other significant events that play a major role in Hindu culture.

About Hindu Deities

Hindu deities are worshipped as both supreme beings and as local spirits. In addition, they are symbols of one or more aspects of nature and are believed to be guardians or upholders of different elements such as land, water, fire, sun, moon, air, and stars. They are often the source of many Hindu laws and principles. Often, they seem to be more powerful than humans, but only because the limitations of humans prevent them from seeing beyond what they can imagine.

This guide will focus on the primary gods and goddesses of the Hindu religion. It will begin with a description of the Brahman, which is one of the most important concepts in Hindu mythology. Next, it will discuss Brahma, who is considered to be one of the principal deities by many Hindus, but not all. Then the guide will progress through detailing Vishnu and Shiva, who are two very powerful Hindu gods, though they are not worshipped by all Hindus. It will conclude with a section on the goddesses of Hinduism, which includes Parvati, the wife of Shiva, Lakshmi, who is Vishnu's consort, and Shakti, who represents the power in reality.

Brahman - The Supreme Reality

The Supreme Reality in Hindu mythology is called Brahman. This reality contains all other realities and gods, but it does not have a specific form or personality. All the manifestations of the Supreme Reality are contained within one form, which has been described as being infinite, beginningless, and endless. In addition to containing all other forms of existence, Vedic literature also describes Brahman as being the ultimate cause of all causes. It is present everywhere in everything, even though it cannot be seen.

In Indian mythology, Brahman encompasses everything that exists in reality and everything beyond physical existence because the Vedic religion recognizes that existence itself is part of a much larger system. In other words, not only does Brahman contain all other realities, but it also explains how those realities exist. For example, Brahman causes a seed to turn into a plant and continues to make up all aspects of that plant, from the root to the leaf. Similarly, everything that exists is an outflow or part of one universal reality that Brahman created.

In addition to being infinite, beginningless, and endless, Brahman is also omniscient. This means that it knows everything about everything everywhere. It knows what exists and what does not exist. It knows the consequences of every action, and it is aware of all things in reality as well as that which is outside of reality. For example, Vedic literature describes how Brahman knows even the thoughts of everyone in existence all at once. At the same time, all manifestations of Brahman are themselves part of the same being.

This unity in diversity is an important aspect of Vedic mythology because it means that one can access Brahman by understanding its perspectives and divisions. A person can know about Brahman by making use of the Vedas, which are a series of texts that contain knowledge about Brahman. The ultimate goal of the Vedas is to provide a means for the believer to return to his or her true self and reunite with Brahman.

Chapter 1: Brahma - Manifestations of the Supreme Reality

Brahma is one of the most popular gods in Hindu mythology. According to Vedic religion, Brahma is one of three manifestations that are part of Brahman. The other two are Vishnu and Shiva. This means that all three have an equal share of power within Brahman, even though they have unique personalities and forms.

Brahma is the manifestation of Brahman that focuses on creation. This means Brahma has power over life and death, as well as all other events resulting from those actions. These abilities make him somewhat similar to a demi-god because his power exceeds humans but is less than the Supreme Reality itself. Brahma is the only god in Hindu mythology who is considered to be a demi-god.

Mythological Depiction

It is important to note that Brahma has four arms. This is significant because it symbolizes his ability to manage all aspects of creation at once. These aspects include time, space, knowledge, and energy. Brahma is typically shown wearing red garments and a turban wrapped around his head. This turban is used to signify that he has complete control over his thoughts and actions, even though he cannot see the future as the Supreme Reality can.

Brahma is often depicted with four faces looking in each direction, including up and down. Having four faces signifies his ability to see everything happening throughout the material and spiritual worlds simultaneously. In addition, he has a fifth face on top of his head, symbolizing supreme knowledge or enlightenment.

Brahma's Symbols

Brahma is associated with the swan. This animal was initially used as a vehicle to help transport him, but it also represents how Brahma has complete control over speech and thought. For example, the swan can separate milk from water and similarly, Brahman can separate truth from falsehood even though those ideas may seem intertwined.

Mythological Stories and Teachings

Brahma's most significant tale is the one that describes how he became aware of his existence. In this story, Brahma begins to wonder why everything in existence has a name except for him, so he decides to search across creation and discover himself. Unfortunately, he becomes tired along the way and rests beneath a fig tree called the Bodhi tree. It is underneath this tree that Brahma becomes enlightened and finally understands why he could not see himself before — because everything in existence was him.

Brahma also has an important role to play in the story of the great god Vishnu. This tale describes how Brahma and Vishnu first met when the Supreme Reality created them both to help restore the balance between good and evil. The two agreed to abide by their mission but, after some time, they decided that the task they had set themselves was too difficult. Neither of them possessed complete dominion over either good or evil because these qualities were all part of the Supreme Reality itself.

Even though their agreement did not last, Brahma and Vishnu became great friends despite their differences. This friendship is highly significant because it suggests that good and evil are completely separate things in Hindu mythology even though they stem from the Supreme Reality. Through this story, we can learn about how good and evil cannot exist without each other and how the Supreme Reality is beyond both of those concepts.

Another story that explains Brahma's significance is the tale of how he sired a daughter with his wife, Gayatri. This daughter was named Sarasvati, and she eventually became the goddess of knowledge and learning in Hindu mythology. Brahma's role in this story is important because it reveals how knowledge and learning are essential to achieving enlightenment.

The Role of Brahma in Hindu Culture

Brahma's role as a creator is highly significant, not only for the people he created but also for the animals from which humans evolved. Some say that during an era of darkness, Brahma transformed into a boar to pull the world from beneath the ocean so that humans could exist. Nowadays, many Hindus worship Brahma as one god even though he is usually seen as one of five forms of the Supreme Reality.

Brahma is not as significant as the other two manifestations of Brahman, but he does play an important role in Vedic religion. It was Brahma who taught the Vedas and their contents to humankind. In addition, Brahma introduced prayer to the world. The prayers were particularly interesting because they allowed individuals to communicate directly with Brahman, a privilege that was previously only available to Brahma himself.

Vedic literature suggests that Brahma also established the four stages of life and created the caste system. The reason for this was to help humans reach enlightenment quicker than they otherwise would have because it would not only let them exist in harmony with each other but also with their environment. The caste system also helped each person understand their place in the world and learn to control their passions and desires.

Brahma's image has influenced Indian culture for hundreds of years and continues to do so today. In most artworks, Brahma is depicted in the meditation pose with four faces and four arms. When he is depicted as such, one face always looks toward the ground to remind people how much Brahma values knowledge and learning even though he was responsible for creating it in the first place.

The role Brahma plays in good and evil is not always important. Sometimes, the stories about him emphasize how he is part of the Supreme Reality instead. The story of his great-granddaughter, Sati, describes how Shiva protected her from an angry Daksha even though she ended up dying after falling into the fire while dancing in front of everyone.

Another story about Brahma occurs after Vishnu is reincarnated as Rama, and he is exiled to the forest for 14 years. During this time, Brahma decides to take some of his creations and turn them into a woman named Sita. After taking her back to heaven with him, Brahma tells Rama that his wife is a magical illusion. In Hindu mythology, this story explains how Sita is the feminine aspect of the Supreme Reality because Brahma created her from nothing.

Brahma is certainly an important god to understand in Hindu mythology, but even though many people worship him as a divine being, his role as a creator is not as significant as the Supreme Reality. Even though many Hindu gods and goddesses play important roles in various stories, Brahma is a bit different because, in many ways, he is simply an aspect of the Supreme Reality.

Chapter 2: Vishnu - The Preserver

Ever since Vishnu fell from the heavenly world of Satyaloka, he has been known as a protector and preserver of good. To restore the balance between good and evil, Vishnu incarnates into different people throughout history because he knows that part of his role is to bring peace and balance to the world.

While his association with good is important, Vishnu's role as a protector is even more significant. In some stories, he saves the world from destruction by taking on various forms and personalities to accomplish his goals. There are many tales about Vishnu that describe how he brings about a balance between good and evil, which is what makes him important to Hindu mythology.

Powers and Abilities of Vishnu

The importance of this god comes from his ability to balance everything out. While Shiva is known as a destroyer and Brahma has the power to create anything he wants, Vishnu represents balance because he destroys things that are too evil and creates things like the world we live in to maintain a perfect balance.

Vishnu's powers are varied and complex, mostly because he is always taking on different forms to save the world. When he appeared as Krishna, Vishnu was considered an avatar of good because everyone loved him. He is also associated with snakes, for some obscure reason, even though there are many stories which tell about how he killed or rescued people from them.

Mythological Depiction of Vishnu

Vishnu was depicted as the wielder of the divine discus even before he appeared as Krishna. The weapon is nothing less than a representation of Vishnu's power because it cuts through anything it touches and is even used to cut up pieces of Satyaloka for people to live on. Traditionally, Vishnu is depicted as blue-skinned and four-armed. Typically, he holds a conch shell, mace, lotus flower, and discus.

The legendary king and warrior Rama is one of the most important depictions of Vishnu. This story tells how Vishnu was incarnated as a human to fight Ravana, who had kidnapped his wife Sita and taken her back to Lanka. After traveling across India for 14 years, along with his brother Lakshmana and an army of monkeys, Rama finally found his way to Lanka. After fighting with Ravana for the return of Sita, Rama killed him and was reunited with his wife in the kingdom of Ayodhya.

Before the god Krishna revealed himself to be a full incarnation of Vishnu, many of his stories were depicted in a different way. Quite often, he was merely a warrior god who helped restore balance to the world after evil people took control. Even though this role of protecting good is still important nowadays, some stories about Vishnu emphasize the wisdom and knowledge he has gained from his many lives.

Vishnu's Role in Hindu Mythology

Vishnu's role in Hindu mythology is significant because he represents the side of good. Even though he is depicted in one of the most important Hindu texts as sleeping for thousands of years, when it comes to protecting and maintaining balance, Vishnu has always been there. One of his most important roles is to save the world from destruction because he knows that true balance comes from good and evil working together.

When it comes to Hindu mythology, there are few gods as well-known as Vishnu. Because he has taken countless different forms throughout history, this god has been a part of many great stories and has even become a staple of Indian culture. Even though Vishnu is associated with good, his balance between good and evil makes him an important god to learn about.

Vishnu's Ten Avatars

Vishnu's avatars are a set of ten different incarnations that all have a specific role to play. While he has taken on many other forms, these particular ten were specifically designed to keep the world from being destroyed.

1. Matsya, the Fish

This was the first avatar in Vishnu's history and appeared when a holy man pleaded for help because there was nothing to protect him at the bottom of the ocean except for his small wooden boat. When he asked for protection, Vishnu turned himself into a fish to guide the man to land where Sankara was performing a fire ceremony. Sankara was so impressed by this act of kindness that he decided to reward the man with moksha, or eternal peace.

2. Kurma the Turtle

Vishnu's second incarnation arrived to help the gods defeat the demons. Even though this form wasn't nearly as popular as some of his other incarnations, it is still worth mentioning because the demons were only able to be defeated when Vishnu turned into a giant turtle that was used as a mountain for them to stand on.

3. Varaha the Boar

After defeating the last set of demons, Vishnu's third avatar manifested to save the earth from being destroyed by an army of demons who had taken over. Vishnu took the form of a boar and fought with their king Hiranyaksha while rescuing his wife.

4. Narsimha

The fourth avatar of Vishnu was Narsimha, a half-man/half-lion creature who saved a man named Prahlada from his evil father. When Prahlada's father decided to kill his son, who he believed was the reincarnation of the Hindu god Vishnu, Narsimha came out of a pillar and slew him with his claws.

5. Vamana, the Dwarf

For Vishnu's fifth incarnation, he appeared as a dwarf and tricked Bali into giving up the real earth by asking for just three paces of land. Each step that Bali took on this new land caused him to lose one of his own steps, which led to him losing all control over it. This form was important because it showed that Vishnu understands how to trick people into revealing their true ignorance.

6. Parasurama

Parasurama was Vishnu's sixth incarnation on earth. He emerged to defeat the evil king Kartavirya, who had gained control over many of India's people with his army. Even though this fight ended in victory for Parasurama, he did end up losing an eye in the process.

7. Rama

As the seventh incarnation of Vishnu, Rama was the hero who slew Ravana and rescued Sita after the demon kidnapped her. The reincarnation of this avatar happened hundreds of years ago in a kingdom named Ayodhya, where Rama was raised to be kind and righteous. He fought against demons throughout his entire life until he was finally able to slay Ravana and reunite with his wife.

8. Krishna

For his eighth incarnation, Vishnu decided to take the form of Krishna to help people. This god ended up becoming a prince and spending much of his life fighting against a demon king named Kamsa in hopes that he could free all of the people from being imprisoned by their ruler.

9. Buddha

Vishnu manifested as a spiritual teacher named Gautama Buddha for his ninth avatar. He came to help people discover themselves. He was an enlightened man who was able to teach others how to be at peace with all aspects of their lives and helped them realize that there is no such thing as an ending because everything can always change.

10.　　Kalki, the Horse

For his last incarnation on earth, Vishnu decided to appear as Kalki the Horse. He is still currently living in heaven until he is eventually sent to Earth with a sword that's meant to destroy all evildoers. Once this happens, Kalki will make sure that the good people are rewarded for their kindness while the bad people will no longer be able to commit evil deeds.

Vishnu's avatars are a way for him to change his appearance on earth to solve problems or help people. He can do this by reincarnating himself as a different being with each generation since the avatar's life always has an impact on those around them. In all of Vishnu's incarnations, he has tried to teach humanity that there is no such thing as an ending because life keeps changing form. This is why Vishnu's avatars are important because they are there to make sure that people are always guided in the right direction.

Chapter 3: Shiva - The God of Destruction

Shiva is the god of destruction for all living things. He creates life by allowing new entities to form out of the existing matter in the universe, but when it's time for them to be reborn into something else, Shiva destroys everything just so that this process can happen again. The destruction he wreaks allows for new creation, which is why all living things on earth worship him by chanting his name.

Shiva's destruction is never the result of animosity or irritation, but rather it is caused by his desire to continuously transform things. He understands that without death, there is no way for life to keep going. Shiva's role as a destroyer is vital because he makes sure that all the changes do not conflict with each other.

Powers and Abilities

Shiva has the power to destroy anything in all of his forms. This means that he can even use his powers on himself when necessary. Shiva's destruction is not limited by time or distance, so nothing can ever escape being destroyed unless it is protected by another god. His ability to create life allows him to control everything within the universe when he is on earth. Shiva does not use his powers to hurt or harm others, but rather he makes sure that all changes are occurring in the way they are supposed to.

Shiva's Attributes

Shiva is usually depicted with either four or six arms, and he can hold multiple objects at once. Some of these objects include a drum, flame, trident, and meditation beads. Shiva's animal gods are snakes because they can move in all directions. He often appears blue and always has a third eye on his forehead.

Shiva lives in the Kailash mountain range and is usually surrounded by fire and snow. He sits upon a tiger skin that's spread across the ground and he sleeps next to his wife named Shakti, who holds a trident in her hand. Shiva is known for having the ability to create many objects out of thin air whenever he needs to. He's also known as Adiyogi, which is a name that means "the first yogi." Shiva has the power to give people anything they want, but he does not let them keep it for long since everything must be destroyed for something new to begin.

Shiva's Stories

There are countless stories about Shiva, many of which deal with his power to destroy and recreate. One such story is about how he was locked in deep meditation at the Kailash mountain range by his son, Ganesha. Shiva remained in this meditative state for more than 100 years, but when he finally awakened, everyone around him was worried because they thought that he had died. The entire universe stopped existing while Shiva was meditating, but when he came back to life from his meditative state, it immediately returned to normal.

Shiva's other story is about how he fell in love with Sati, the daughter of Daksha. Daksha didn't like Shiva because he wanted his daughter to marry someone who would be more beneficial for their family name, so he said that she could only marry a man who was more handsome than Shiva. Sati didn't agree with Daksha's new terms because she loved Shiva, so she decided to make the ultimate sacrifice by jumping into a sacrificial fire and killing herself. She died from her wounds before anyone could save her from this fate, but when Shiva heard what happened, he became very angry. He started a war against everyone who was responsible for Sati's death, but when they all died, he realized that there was nothing left in his life without Sati. Shiva decided to carry her body with him everywhere since it had become a part of him when she died, and this caused him to be forever known as Ardhanari.

One of Shiva's most popular stories is about how he saved the universe from being destroyed by fire. Two demons known as Andhaka and Halahala had decided to fight against the gods because they wanted world domination. The battle between them escalated so quickly that it ended up filling the entire universe with fire. Just when it seemed like the entire universe was lost, Shiva came to save everyone. He swallowed up all of the fire that was burning within Andhaka's body, which filled his throat until it was completely blocked. This caused Shiva to turn blue and remain in this state for years until he finally released the fire back into the universe.

Shiva is often seen as being one of the more misunderstood gods because he doesn't want to be worshipped or praised for his powers. Instead, he wants people to understand that everything must come in cycles. Shiva stays inside his mountain and rarely interacts with mortals, and when he does, it's always for a very specific reason. He can give people whatever they want, but he does not do this simply to please them since it would be an insult to their intelligence. Shiva wants everyone to understand that there are only so many things in the world, and once one of these things is gone, it will never return without being replaced by something else.

Chapter 4: Ganesha - The God with the Elephant Head

Ganesha is one of the most popular gods in Hindu mythology because he's considered to be the lord of success and destroyer of evil. Ganesha was worshiped by several different religions before humans knew that they all referred to the same god. This led to him being known as "the god without a beginning."

Ganesha is the only god in Hindu mythology who had a human experience before becoming a god, which is something that makes him stand out from all the other deities. There are many different things about Ganesha's story that make him special, but perhaps one of his best-known attributes is that he has the head of an elephant. Ganesha has a beautiful human body, and his head is like that because he loves spending time outdoors, surrounded by nature. This makes it easy for him to create friendships with many different animals.

Ganesha's head was not originally shaped like that of an elephant's. One story says that the goddess Parvati asked Ganesha to stand guard while she took a bath. While Parvati was taking her time to bathe, Shiva came back home and was stopped by Ganesha from entering the house. Shiva got angry and cut off Ganesha's head, which made Parvati very upset. She told Shiva to fix this problem by replacing Ganesha's head with the first thing that he saw, which was an elephant. The gods were so impressed by Ganesha's commitment that they blessed him so that he became the first god that people would pray to receive anything they wanted.

Ganesha's Powers

Ganesha is known to be a very powerful god because he was given the title "lord of success," and he has also been given the power to be able to remove all obstacles in life. His blessings are so powerful that they can make any wish come true. Because of this, people often pray to him if their prayers aren't answered by other gods. Ganesha is known for having a very kind heart, which is why he's always willing to help anyone who asks for his help.

Attributes

Ganesha is often depicted as being a very tall and muscular god because he's known for being a great dancer who loves music. He's always seen wearing bright, yellow-colored clothes, which add to his overall charm. Ganesha has the head of an elephant upon a much larger human body, and this is why he is also known as "the elephant god." Ganesha can be found holding objects in his standard four arms, but he can grow more arms whenever he needs to.

Tales of Ganesha's Greatness

There are many different tales told about Ganesha in Hindu mythology because he is known for being a very wise and intelligent god. One story tells of how Ganesha was able to write the Mahabharata, which is an ancient Indian epic poem that's considered to be one of the greatest literary works in history. In this story, Ganesha managed to write the entire epic poem in only one day because he had more than thirty-three thousand extra hands to help him with this task.

Another story tells of how Ganesha taught humans how they were supposed to live their lives. In this tale, it is said that several gods and goddesses decided to live as humans so that they could learn from their mistakes. Ganesha was the only god who didn't want to do this because he felt it would be a bad idea, but after seeing how much everyone wanted to be human, he decided to become a human himself. He did this by only eating the food that was given to him and never drinking any water because he wanted to know what it would feel like to live without water and sourcing/making his own food.

Ganesha learned that it was much more difficult to live as a human than he thought because there were so many different struggles that people had to deal with. After seeing how hard it was for them to live in this way, Ganesha used what he had learned from his experience and told everyone else what they should be doing.

Ganesha is also known as Vinayaka. Hindus pray to Ganesha before starting any new activity, and they also pray to him if they want their wishes to come true. He is known as the remover of obstacles, which makes it easy for people to remove anything that's standing in their way by simply praying to Ganesha. This god believes in helping humans without expecting anything in return because he believes that good karma comes back to him when he helps others.

Many Hindu mythology stories are based on tales known as the Puranas. These are ancient stories that were written down to help people learn about their culture's beliefs. Because one of the main purposes of these stories was to teach people how they should be living their lives, most of them had a moral message that they were urged to glean and embody. The story of Ganesha demonstrates this because it shows us that all of his greatness came from the fact that he was willing to learn from his mistakes.

Chapter 5: Hanuman - The Monkey God

Hanuman is a male deity that's known for being the great hero featured in the Hindu epic poem, Ramayana. He was born as a demi-god which means that he was half-god and half-human, and he had supernatural powers because of this. Hanuman spent his life helping those in need, and he is known for being a kind, compassionate, and brave individual who always stood up for what he believed was right.

Lord Hanuman has the appearance of a monkey, but he is usually described as being human-like in most other ways. He has large eyes and ears that are symbolically linked to the Hindu god Rama, who is another important deity within Hindu mythology. Because of Hanuman's great love for Rama, his eyes and ears were always very large so that he could pay attention to him at all times.

People who pray to Lord Hanuman are often hoping to receive help to overcome obstacles, and they feel as though he can provide them with positive energy that will push them forward. This god gives people the strength that they need to deal with any kind of problems that may be holding them back from being who they want to be or preventing them from doing what they're passionate about. Many Hindus believe that Lord Hanuman is the perfect role model for this kind of behavior because he always stood up for what was right, no matter what people thought about him.

Hanuman's Powers and Abilities

Hanuman was known for being a shape-shifter, which means that he was able to change his physical form so that he could live life as any type of animal. He usually preferred to remain in the form of a monkey because this was the creature that most resembled him, and it allowed Hanuman to accomplish things that were beyond the capabilities of a human. Most people tend to think of Hanuman as being a monkey because this is how he is most commonly shown in images and statues, but he can also take other forms if needed.

Hanuman had many magical powers, and the first one that usually comes to mind relates to his superhuman strength. He was known for traveling incredibly fast since he could fly through the air, and he mainly used this power to get himself where he needed to go more quickly than any person could walk or run. His great speed is also shown through his ability to travel over very long distances in just a single jump, and this power helped him get to any place that he so desired without having to go the long way around. Hanuman has been known for using these abilities to help those who may be suffering or struggling with difficult circumstances so that he can offer them some kind of assistance.

Hanuman is described as being a very intelligent and wise figure, and he's also known for having great strength. All of these traits came from the fact that he was born with an incredible level of self-confidence that never seemed to waver. He could jump many, many miles into the air without any kind of injury or side effects because he was very certain that he could do it. Hanuman was also able to accomplish all of his tasks because he believed that he could do anything as long as it was for the benefit of others. As you can see, Hanuman's power came from within even though his physical abilities were what set him apart from other demi-gods.

Hanuman's Role in Hindu Mythology

Hanuman is known as being one of the most important figures in Hindu mythology. He is often described as being invincible. Hanuman was also the perfect embodiment of Rama's ideals because he exhibited many traits that were symbolic of this deity. This god has been depicted in art and literature as a brave hero with a great deal of physical strength. Hanuman was also known for being Rama's most loyal friend, and he never wavered in his service to him no matter what obstacles got in their way.

Hanuman has often been described as being an ideal example of the perfect disciple, and this phrase is used quite frequently in the Hindu faith. He is described as being selfless, humble, and willing to do whatever was necessary to serve his god without complaint or hesitation. Hanuman also displayed a great deal of wisdom because he always used this quality when making decisions on behalf of the entire world.

This demi-god has been depicted in art with multiple heads and arms and was shown with the most appropriate number of limbs for any given circumstance. The Hindu god Rama has been found in many historical texts and other forms of art, but he is almost always accompanied by his favorite disciple Hanuman.

The Modern Era

Hanuman remains an important figure in Hindu mythology, but he also plays a very active role in modern society. Many people tend to use his image when they are wearing clothing that features various Hindu god-themed styles, and he has become quite a popular tattoo design.

Hanuman is still worshiped by many devout Hindus because he is seen as being the symbol of physical strength and power. This demi-god has been used to set an example to others who are looking to live their lives in a way that is noble, honorable, and selfless. Hanuman's powers have also been seen as being symbolic representations of the inner strength that everyone possesses within themselves. The idea behind this symbolism is that anyone can achieve greatness so long as they believe in themselves and work towards some kind of common goal that benefits those around them.

Chapter 6: Laxmi - The Goddess of Fortune

Laxmi is the Hindu goddess of fortune, which means that she is responsible for keeping track of everyone's good and bad luck. She also has the power to grant people's wishes so long as they can provide her with an offering in return. When someone gains wealth or finds themselves coming into a large sum of money, it is said to be because Laxmi was looking favorably upon them and decided to assist. The goddess has been known for blessing those who are willing to live their lives following her ideals so that she will keep helping them out whenever they ask her.

Laxmi's Origins

The Hindu goddess Laxmi has been worshiped for centuries, and her appearance as a deity only varies slightly from one tradition to the next. She is always seen as being important within Hindu mythology because she is associated with Rama's other half, Sita. Laxmi was used as a representation of everything that Sita should have been during this period, and this symbolism is very important because it shows how much she was revered by religious devotees of that era.

Laxmi's character also holds a great deal of importance to modern women because her narrative illustrates what it means to be a good wife, mother, and daughter-in-law. The goddess had many different roles that were designed to make her very appealing to other Hindu women who were looking for an example of how they should live their lives.

The worship of Laxmi has continued well into the modern era, and many women still find her to be a source of inspiration because she is seen as being one of the most important goddesses of the Hindu faith. The symbolism behind this religion's goddesses has been very helpful to women who are trying to learn more about the role that they should be playing in society. In many cases, the symbolism has been able to provide women with a way to see themselves as being similar to the goddesses of this faith.

Laxmi's Symbolic Aspects

The primary way in which Laxmi has been able to provide women with a sense of inspiration is through the symbolism that she uses to illustrate her role as a goddess. She is often shown holding many different kinds of objects that are associated with wealth, fertility, and good fortune. In some cases, she has been known to hold a lotus flower, which is an important part of many Hindu traditions because it symbolizes new beginnings. The lotus flower also represents purity and beauty, which are two concepts that can also be associated with Laxmi.

Laxmi has been shown holding the gem known as the Kaustubha, which is associated with Rama. The gem was said to have been brought forth from Vishnu's chest by none other than Laxmi herself. This symbolizes how she can guide people toward a path of righteousness while also keeping good track of everyone's moral choices.

In some instances, the Hindu goddess Laxmi was also shown as having four arms. This is another important part of her symbolic aspect because Hindus believe that the number four holds a great deal of importance. Four represents the four Vedas, which are ancient Hindu texts that are thought to contain knowledge about proper behavior and conduct. This symbolism has been important because it reinforces the idea that Laxmi is looking at each devotee equally so that she can reward them for properly following her way of life if they should choose to do so.

Laxmi's Attributes

Laxmi is known for being extremely kind and generous because she will do whatever she can to help others gain wealth or find good fortune during their lives. The goddess is often seen as a symbol of prosperity, and many people attempt to please her when they are looking for ways to become wealthy. Laxmi is also known for being very gentle because she likes to look at the good qualities in each person rather than dwelling on their negative aspects.

Laxmi's appearance varies significantly from one tradition to the next, but she is often thought to be very beautiful and graceful. She is known for having long black hair that is often tied in a braid, and she wears expensive jewelry on her body that makes her look like royalty. The goddess has been described as wearing red or golden robes that are covered in jewels, which represent the beauty of the natural world even though she is often seen as being detached from it.

Laxmi is also thought to be very intelligent and skillful, which means that she has the knowledge and wisdom required to provide people with all of the riches that they could hope for during their lives. Laxmi has also been known to demonstrate patience when it comes to people's mistakes. This is because she understands that every person has the chance to turn their lives around and become just as wealthy as they could hope for.

Laxmi's Role in Hinduism

Laxmi is very similar to many of the other Hindu goddesses because she has the power to provide people with anything that they could ever want or need. She can do this because she is associated with Vishnu, who is known as being the god of preservation and sustenance. Laxmi balances out Vishnu's role perfectly because she can give people what they are looking for in life.

The concept of Lakshmi has existed for many centuries, and it can be traced back to an ancient tradition known as Vaishnavism. The goddess is often known as being shy and modest. She also has a soft spot for musicians, and many people make statues of her with one hand raised as if she is attempting to ward off evil. This is because Lakshmi cannot stand trouble, which means that she can be very protective when it comes to looking after all worshippers who are devoted to her cause.

Lakshmi has become an extremely popular goddess throughout the world because she is the woman who everyone looks up to when they are trying to gain wealth or material possessions during their lives. The Hindu deity is known for having many different associations in the world, and she is thought to come from a long line of goddesses that have been worshipped throughout the years.

Chapter 7: Agni - The God of Fire

The Hindu god Agni is known for being the personification of fire, which means that he represents both the destructive and purifying aspects of this natural force. He is the son of the god of space and ruler of the earth, Varuna, which means that he is also known to represent many other natural forces like lightning and storms. Agni has no consort because he is associated with both life-giving and death-dealing fire.

People often compare Agni to being a messenger of the gods because he can travel between the material world and the heavens so easily. He has been known as being completely unbiased. He will not look at people's social status or caste when he is trying to determine if they are worthy enough for him to carry one of their prayers. Agni has been compared to being a caretaker who can provide people with wealth and prosperity in life because he is known for having the ability to rescue people from all of the dangers that surround them.

Agni's Role in Hinduism

Agni is believed to be the god of many different things, and he has been worshipped as being the lord of all fire for centuries. He is thought to be a messenger from the other side because he can travel through the spiritual plane that joins people with their ancestors. Agni is known by many names that reflect his importance in Hinduism, including God of Fire, Purifier, and Embodiment of Light.

Agni has been used to represent the divine force that comes from within people during different religious ceremonies, including weddings. His presence is often invoked in these situations because he can destroy everything, such as bad influences, and transform them into something entirely new and fresh. Agni can also provide people with wealth and prosperity when they require these things because he is associated with the power that enables this change to happen.

Agni is often worshipped during different Vedic rituals, which means that he has played an important role in making these events successful since the very beginning of Hinduism. The god's presence is invoked at different significant milestones, and he has been worshipped as a household deity for just as long. People often rely on Agni to provide them with warmth and light when they are living their daily lives because he represents the fire inside of everyone's hearts that allows hope and belief to blossom in dark times.

The Origins of Agni

There are many different stories about how Agni was first created, but the most popular one states that he was first brought into existence during a time when Brahma and Vishnu were resting on the serpent Ananta. It is believed that the two powerful beings wanted to create some sort of entity that could maintain all the celestial fires in the universe, and Agni was brought into existence as he traveled through the spiritual realm.

During this time, it is said that Vishnu had fallen asleep for a very long period before he awoke to see that his brothers were fighting with each other because of their ongoing rivalry. The god decided to intervene by appearing before both of them as human beings, but it is said that they continued to fight because they could not recognize him. Vishnu then grew tired of their bickering and decided that he needed to create a new form for himself that would reflect all of the different aspects of his personality.

It is believed that after Vishnu had created this new form, he saw that one of its hands had been fashioned into a shape that resembled a closed lotus. The god is said to have realized that if this hand was clenched tightly, it would represent Brahma's intense desire to create something new and fresh in the universe. If the same hand was opened with all five fingers spread out, then it would reflect Vishnu's ability to destroy everything to start over again.

The god decided that he was not satisfied with this image, but when he tried to make further changes, it is said that the other hand moved up to his shoulder and blocked him from seeing anything else. This hand ended up becoming Brahma's gift for Agni so that he could help to destroy everything to bring something new into the universe.

Agni's Role in Vedic Rituals

Agni is often used during different Vedic rituals because he has the power to purify items, people, and places as he moves through them. In these situations, some Hindus will place a fire burning on a brick or some other type of elevated surface as they attempt to burn away impurities that exist in their lives. This is because these people believe that Agni can enter them and cleanse them by destroying all negative influences, including bad karma that could prevent their spiritual development.

If people can create the right conditions, it is said that Agni will present them with special offerings during their spiritual quests. These offerings include things like ghee, milk, sesame seeds, and other types of food that have been prepared through fasting. This process is believed to help people become closer to god so that they can enjoy a deeper connection with him over time.

Agni is also used during various funeral rituals because he plays a critical role in ensuring that people's ancestors can move on to the afterlife once their bodies have decomposed. During these instances, it is believed that Agni enters the corpse of the deceased and brings it back to life so that they can travel through the spiritual realm and gain the wisdom they need to continue their growth. Agni performs a reverse role in this process by taking them back into his mouth and removing everything that is no longer needed so that the cycle of rebirth can begin again.

Agni is believed to have been born from a lotus that emerged from the navel of Vishnu while his brothers were bickering. He is often called upon during spiritual events because he has the power to purify people and remove negative influences from their lives. This purification often involves burning away bad karma or negative karmic influences so that people can continue to grow and develop. Agni is also believed to help the souls of people move into the afterlife, where they can gain wisdom through their journeys there.

Chapter 8: Saraswati - The Goddess of Learning

Goddess Saraswati is the Hindu deity of knowledge, music, arts, and science. She symbolizes the power of Brahma. Saraswati is also called Bharati or Vak Devi, goddess of speech. As per Hindu belief, she was born to sage Kashyap and his wife, Aditi. She is the divine consort of Lord Brahma, with whom she is said to have fathered four Kumaras. Saraswati is also known as Vani and Vagdevi.

In Hinduism, Saraswati is regarded as the mother of the Vedas. The word 'Saraswati' evolved from 'sara' and 'swa,' meaning "essence" and "one who dwells," respectively. Thus, Saraswati means "the essence of the self-existing knowledge." She is also called Jagadgauri, "the one who is radiant everywhere in the world."

Saraswati's Symbolism

Saraswati is often depicted as a beautiful woman dressed in pure white who is seated on a swan or a white lotus, both of which symbolize her purity. In some traditions, she has four hands, each carrying an object that symbolizes one of the four goals of human life considered important to the Hindu culture. The four objects are a book representing knowledge, a musical instrument representing harmony, a string of prayer beads representing devotion to God, and pomegranates or lotuses, representing fertility.

Saraswati is also often shown teaching Brahma, who is seated at her feet in the lotus position. Saraswati's association with white or pure colors represents her purity. She is believed to be the energy that runs through all the chakras in a person's body.

Saraswati's association with the swan also symbolizes discrimination between good and bad and purity of thought. Saraswati is believed to be one of seven elements (or Tattvas) of primal matter (Prakriti). The other six elements are fire, earth, space/ether, water, air, and ahamkara (ego).

In the Vedas

In Hindu mythology, Saraswati is regarded as the river from which all knowledge manifests. She gives inspiration to all artists who practice their art with devotion. Her blessings are invoked before the beginning of any ceremony or festival. She is hailed as the giver of true knowledge (vidya), which frees people from all fear and suffering. Saraswati is also equated with the power of speech. In Hindu tradition, knowledge and spiritual liberation are achieved through the correct utterance of a mantra or sacred words. Saraswati is revered as the goddess of learning in schools and temples. She blesses all students who enter these temples with an abundance of knowledge, creativity, artistic skills, and musical abilities.

Saraswati in Art and Literature

Sculptures of Saraswati depict her with four arms, usually playing the veena (a lute-like instrument), symbolizing her role in composing Vedic hymns. Her vahana or vehicle is a white swan wearing jewels on its beak. In artwork, she often wears white and gold-colored silk garments.

Saraswati is the goddess who gave Indian artists the knowledge of fine arts such as sculpture, painting, drama, music composition, and poetry. She also inspired musicians such as Tansen, one of the Nine Jewels of Emperor Akbar's court. He was considered the most outstanding musician in the court of Akbar. According to legend, Saraswati gave him music lessons in exchange for Tansen's promise that he would build a temple dedicated to her.

Saraswati in Yoga

According to the Hindu Yogis, Saraswati is the presiding deity of intellect. Saraswati is also regarded as one of five major deities whose energy forms an integral part of every human being. Each of these five deities represents a particular aspect of life, and each has a color that corresponds to it. Saraswati's color is white, which represents the "fifth state" of existence called "Turiya" or pure consciousness. The other four deities are Brahma (red), Shiva (dark or blue-green), Vishnu (golden, like the sun), and Devi (black).

Saraswati is also associated with Kundalini Shakti, the spiritual energy that lies dormant at the base of the spine. When this shakti rises through the six chakras or centers of spiritual power, it eventually reaches the crown chakra, revealing true knowledge to the aspirant. Saraswati is known as the mother of the Vedas. She is also considered a symbol of self-realization and a representation of a person's highest potential.

Saraswati's Role in Hindu Life

An important worship ceremony dedicated to Saraswati takes place every year on Vasant Panchami day in January-February. This festival is also referred to as Saraswati Puja. On this day, statues and paintings of Saraswati are worshiped and decorated with flowers and festoons, in schools and temples all over India. Books, musical instruments, and art pieces used for decoration also form an integral part of the festival. This day commemorates the day Shiva handed over the divine lute to King Vishnu as a gift for his consort, Parvati. This event symbolizes music's role in worship and prayer.

Hindu tradition states that it is Saraswati's power that enables a woman to express herself through music, culture, song, and creative literature. Thus, both men and women honor the goddess by dedicating themselves to these arts. Saraswati is often invoked in Hindu rituals for purification, the blessing of offerings, removal of evil influences, and prosperity. Hindus also pray to Saraswati for knowledge in the arts and sciences, wisdom, intelligence, musical abilities, skill at their profession or craft, and pure thoughts.

Chapter 9: Durga - The Goddess of Power

Goddess Durga is the fiercest form of Devi, the mother goddess. She was created by the Divine Mother for a specific purpose, which explains her wrathful nature. Once, when all of the gods were being tortured by a demon named Mahishasura, they sought help from Devi. She agreed to help them and hunted this demon. To give her more power, each of the gods gave Durga a piece of themself. The result was an awesome and ferocious form that killed the demon, revealing to them and the world the true power of the feminine aspect of Brahman.

Durga is often depicted riding a tiger or lion and carrying a trident in one hand and a lotus flower in the other hand. She is seated on a lotus, which represents the power of her enlightened heart. In some images, she is shown as an ordinary woman who has emerged from a fiery pillar. The seven children that she holds in some depictions represent the Seven Rays or Chakras, through which Kundalini passes as it rises through the spine to reveal pure consciousness at the Crown Chakra. Durga has also been credited with slaying three demons or evil forces that reside in the human body which include ego, pride, and lust. It is said that these demons keep humans from experiencing their true divine nature.

Durga's Symbolism and Spiritual Meaning

Durga represents the transformation of raw, untamed energy into refined and focused power. She is often referred to as the "Divine Mother" and is venerated throughout India for her nurturing nature. According to Hindu legend, it was because of Durga's protection that Lord Rama was able to defeat Ravana and release Sita from captivity.

Durga's powers are said to be limitless. She is the ruler of time, space, and consciousness. Durga rides on a lion or tiger to symbolize her ability to rise above worldly challenges with courage and grace. Her weapons include a selection of swords, maces, arrows, axes, bows, and other deadly instruments that enable her to defeat any enemy.

Durga's worship is considered auspicious for the fulfillment of worldly desires and success. She bestows tremendous strength that can be used both destructively and constructively. Durga is sometimes referred to by other names, including Uma, Bhavani, and Kali. She has many arms that represent the many aspects of consciousness that need to be mastered for us to achieve spiritual awareness. Thus, she can give us guidance and inspiration when we find ourselves struggling with more than one task at a time. Durga is also often depicted with eight or ten arms to signify that she can respond to many challenges simultaneously.

Durga is believed to cure diseases of the body and mind, especially those related to egoism. She helps her devotees exceed the limitations they have set for themselves. Durga represents both beauty and power. The lotus she carries symbolizes purity because it moves up through muddy waters but emerges spotless due to its ability to draw water away. The animal on which she rides represents her ability to understand and master the world.

Durga's Role in Hindu Life

Durga's worshipers believe that she bestows the power to overcome obstacles, especially those related to ego and pride. In Hinduism, these two qualities are considered grave impediments to spiritual growth because they cover up our innate wisdom and prevent us from seeing things as they truly are. Durga helps her devotees to discern their true essence and to overcome the false sense of limitation that they have created for themselves.

Durga is often mentioned in Sanskrit hymns and Puranas. She is highly respected and worshipped by both Hindus and Buddhists. Although she has a relatively limited role in Hindu mythology, she is a/the central character in many stories, including those of Lord Rama's battle against the demon-king Ravana. Durga represents the power of pure consciousness as well as spiritual wisdom. She helps her devotees understand their true, divine nature. She represents both beauty and might, which may be exploited for either positive or negative results.

Durga is a powerful goddess who removes the veil of limitation that hides our true essence from us. She represents the power to overcome any worldly challenge as well as the obstacles that prevent us from knowing ourselves. This goddess has been known to cure diseases, including those of pride and egoism, which are considered impediments to spiritual growth.

Durga's Forms and Attributes

1. Maha Gauri: The White Goddess

Maha Gauri is usually shown riding a white tiger and wearing spotless white garments. She holds a bowl of nectar that symbolizes the benefits she bestows upon her devotees. Her complexion is fair, representing purity and wisdom.

2. Maha Kali: The Fierce Protector

According to Hindu stories, Kali is black and rides a black tigress. She holds a "Khatvanga" (a club with a skull at the top of it) for her weapon, which bestows upon its targets the fear of death. Kali's dark complexion signifies her ability to absorb any darkness that exists within us.

3. Maha Lakshmi: The Fulfilling One

Maha Lakshmi is the epitome of beauty and good fortune. She has golden skin, which represents her mastery over wealth, knowledge, and prosperity. As Lakshmi's power is manifested in the material world, she is most often worshipped by those who wish to obtain worldly things such as happiness, comfort, success, and good fortune.

Myths and Stories Involving Durga

The Power of Consciousness

Durga is at the center of many Hindu myths and stories because she represents pure, divine consciousness, also known as Shakti. During the battle against evil, Lord Shiva takes the form of a fierce warrior who is believed to embody pure masculine potential. As he battles the demons with his unbridled fury, Lord Shiva becomes so immersed in his energy that he loses sight of the entire battlefield. It is during this time that Durga reveals herself and realizes her true nature as consciousness. She emerges from within Lord Shiva's fierce energy to remind him of his duty as a destroyer and nurturer. She shows him his true role on the battlefield, which is to transform negative forces into positive ones so that life may be able to continue on earth uninterrupted.

The Demons' Defeat at Durga's Hands

Durga ultimately defeats Mahishasura through her divine wisdom, feminine beauty, and might. She shows the demons that there is no need to fear death because after death comes to another form of life. Durga grows to be like a mother at the end of her fight with Mahishasura, treating the demons who sought to destroy her in the same way as a mother would treat her children.

The Gods' Defeat

The defeat of Indra and the other gods by a demon named Bala enhances Durga's power. Indra and the others fear that they have become too complacent as protectors of heaven, so they pray to Lord Shiva for help. In return for being rescued from certain doom, Indra promises loyalty to Lord Shiva and pledges his full support to him. This event strengthens the bond between Durga and Lord Shiva, as well as his devotion to her.

According to Hindu stories, Durga is considered to be the most powerful goddess of all. In some stories, she is even called the Supreme Being because she symbolizes the active expression of Shakti. Durga is a brave and skillful fighter who fights to protect her followers from evil forces. She holds a special place in the hearts of Hindus because she embodies the ability to overcome dark forces by using our inner strength to withstand any challenge that may come our way.

Chapter 10: Indra - The Mighty Storm

Indra is the god of thunder, lightning, storms, rains, and water. He is one of the most important deities in the Hindu religion. He represents honor, masculine virility and is mostly considered to be a warrior or fighter. Indra is said to have been born from a lotus flower that grew from Vishnu's navel. He is the leader of the Devas and one of the most powerful gods in Hinduism.

Indra's mother, Aditi, is the goddess of the sky, and his father is Dyaus Pita (also known as "Heaven"). After Indra was born, he gained control over all of the gods and goddesses in Hinduism. He is also known as King of Heaven or King of all the gods. Indra's other titles are Arjuna, One with beautiful locks of hair, Slayer of Vritra, Slayer of Paka, Destroyer of cities, Mighty ruler.

Indra is also considered to be one of the Trimurti. The Trimurti is a group of three gods in Hinduism. These three gods consist of Brahma, Vishnu, and Shiva. He represents thunder and storms and is said to bring fertility wherever he reigns through his power over rainbows, lightning, and thunder.

Indra's Symbolism

In addition to being the god of storms, thunder, and rain, Indra is also the god of fertility and harvest. As a result, he is considered to be one of the most powerful gods in Hinduism. Indra's domain is in heaven with his wife Indrani, which makes him an important figure for those who practice Hinduism.

As a storm god, Indra's weapon is the vajra or thunderbolt, which was created from a tree on Vishnu's chest. Sometimes he is depicted as riding an elephant called Airavata throughout Hindu epics and stories, which also connects him to rain because elephants are known for being able to swim in the water. He is also known as a generous god by providing resources to those who need them and helping others fight against demons.

Indra as a Storm God

Vajra, Indra's thunderbolt, is used to create rain and storms that destroy evil forces. He uses this weapon throughout the epics to lead the other gods against the forces of evil.

Indra takes pleasure in fighting demons, who are followers of Vritra. Vritra was an evil demon who is said to be the manifestation of drought. He causes a season-long drought by hiding all of the water and rain of the world in a cave, which causes a famine for many people.

Indra defeats Vritra by releasing this water from its cave and then killing Vritra with his thunderbolt. As a result, he brings back fertility to the land by causing rain that makes crops grow again. Vritra is also considered to be one of Indra's ancestors, but he tried to overthrow his rule over heaven many times in Hinduism's history. This led the gods and goddesses to fight against him to protect their king.

Indra's Relationship with the Other Gods

When Indra is depicted in Hindu epics, he is usually shown alongside his wife Indrani, also known as Sachi. The two are considered to be very close and live together in heaven. During this time, he also becomes friends with other gods such as Lord Vishnu and Lord Shiva.

Indra becomes enemies with other gods such as the Asuras (demons), who are led by their king called Vritra. Indra comes to blows with the demons after helping the Devas to overthrow them and gain control of heaven. He also has a rivalry with many wind gods throughout Hinduism's history, which makes sense because Indra is a storm god who represents thunder and rain.

The Hindu mythological tales depict Indra as being extremely generous to the gods when they are in need or fight against demons to protect their honor. He is often depicted as a great king who cares for his people and supporters by providing them with the necessary resources they need.

Indra and Trimurti

Images of Indra are usually shown alongside other Hindu gods such as Lord Vishnu and Lord Shiva, which connects him to the Trimurti of today's Hinduism. There is a story about how Indra obtained his status as one of the Trimurti and also about his great power. In this story, Indra kills a demon who had obtained the boon of being able to be killed only by an omniscient (all-knowing) god. After Indra kills him, Vishnu tells Indra that he can choose any boon as a reward for his actions. Indra asks to be the most powerful god in Hinduism, which Vishnu grants him as a reward.

Indra and his wife Indrani are part of the Trimurti through Lord Vishnu, who is known as a creator god in Hindu epics and stories. Indra's domain is within heaven with his wife Indrani, which is similar to that of Lord Shiva. Lord Shiva has the domain within the material realm, which is known as Earth. Vishnu's domain was said to be in between heaven and Earth because he led many Hindu epics with his avatars or incarnations, such as Rama and Krishna.

Vedic Indra vs. Puranic Indra

The Vedic Indra is very different from the Puranic Indra. The Vedic Indra was said to be a mighty warrior and led many wars against demons such as Vritra, who was his main enemy in Hindu tales. He also had many affairs with other goddesses, such as Ushas (goddess of dawn) and Svadha (goddess of the departed).

In contrast, the Puranic Indra was said to be a representation of happiness and joy. He was also said to be a representation of good luck. He is usually depicted with his wife Indrani, who is a goddess herself who represents luck and beauty. In some Hindu epics, such as the Ramayana, Indra's status within the Trimurti rises from simply being one of three gods to becoming Lord Vishnu's main son.

Indra is a Hindu rain god who is known for his great power, strength, and generosity toward the other gods. He came to power along with his wife Indrani by overthrowing demons that invaded heaven to gain control of it. The two are considered very close in Hinduism's history. Indra has many skills which make him a powerful god with great strength, which include his ability to see into the future. He is also known for being very generous toward the other gods in terms of providing them with their necessary resources.

Conclusion

Hindu Mythology is a subject that evokes interest. It reflects the spiritual and cultural heritage of India. In this guide to the gods and goddesses of Hindu Mythology, we have covered the history of Hindu Mythology and explained many aspects of this vast subject.

In Hindu Mythology, all living creatures are believed to be a part of Brahman. It is believed that the whole world takes place as a result of Brahman, the supreme power. This guide talked about the creation of nature and its creatures, which ultimately resulted in the creation of Man. Hindu mythology explains that there are thirty-three core gods in the Hindu pantheon. These include the Trimurti, or the three main gods of Hindu mythology, namely Brahma, Vishnu, and Shiva. All other deities are believed to be manifestations of these three primary gods.

Brahma is believed to be the creator of all that exists. He is also regarded as the primary god in Hindu mythology. Brahma is depicted with four heads and carries a scepter made of sugarcane, which he uses for initiation ceremonies. Vishnu is considered to be the preserver of nature and all its creatures. It was Vishnu who used his divine powers of preservation and re-creation to save the world from destruction. Shiva is the destroyer in Hindu mythology and one of the Trimurti. He represents all that is new and fresh, while Brahma and Vishnu represent what has been. As Shiva is also known as Bholenath, he is often worshipped in the form of an ordinary man.

Apart from these three major deities, other Hindu gods and goddesses also play important roles in Hindu beliefs. Rama and Krishna are revered as Avatars, or incarnations, of Vishnu, while Durga and Kali represent Shakti. Many other gods and goddesses also occupy a significant position in the great Hindu epics. Ganesha, Parvati, Saraswati, Surya, Lakshmi, Indra, Agni, and Hanuman are some of these prominent deities. Besides being the basis of every virtue and principle in Hindu culture, these characters have a very interesting background and a specific role to play in Hindu Mythology.

References

Adhikari, S. (2015, December 15). Top 10 interesting facts about Hindu mythology. Ancienthistorylists.Com. https://www.ancienthistorylists.com/india-history/top-10-interesting-hindu-mythology/

Beliefs. (n.d.). BBC. Retrieved from https://www.bbc.co.uk/religion/religions/hinduism/beliefs/intro_1.shtml

Hindu gods and goddesses - dummies. (2016, March 26). Dummies.Com. https://www.dummies.com/religion/hinduism/hindu-gods-and-goddesses/

Hinduism and Mythology. (n.d.). Mythencyclopedia.Com. Retrieved from http://www.mythencyclopedia.com/Go-Hi/Hinduism-and-Mythology.html

Mandal, D. (2018, September 18). Major Hindu gods, goddesses, and their family tree. Realmofhistory.Com. https://www.realmofhistory.com/2018/09/18/major-hindu-gods-goddesses-facts/

The Most Important Hindu Gods: Shiva - Vishnu - Brahma - Hanuman - Ganesha - Vol 1- see U in History. (2020, July 13). YouTube. https://www.youtube.com/watch?v=ZQz-OxTqlTc

www.ingramcontent.com/pod-product-compliance
Lightning Source LLC
Chambersburg PA
CBHW071237130726
47998CB00003B/993